THE LOST CITY OF ATLANTIS

Natalie Hyde

CRABTREE
Publishing Company
www.crabtreebooks.com

Crabtree Publishing Company
www.crabtreebooks.com

Author: Natalie Hyde
**Publishing plan research
    and development**: Reagan Miller
Project coordinator: Crystal Sikkens
Editors: Sonya Newland, Crystal Sikkens
Proofreader: Janine Deschenes
Designer: Tim Mayer
Map: Stefan Chabluk
Cover design: Ken Wright
**Production coordinator and
    prepress technician**: Ken Wright
Print coordinator: Margaret Amy Salter
Production coordinated by:
    White-Thomson Publishing

Photographs:
Alamy: Christian Darkin; pp. 16–17; North Wind
Picture Archives: p. 32; Montagu Images: p. 35;
AF Archive: pp. 42–43; Bridgeman Art Library:
Solon giving laws to the Greeks, 6th Century BC
(chromolitho), French School, (19th century)/Private
Collection/© Look and Learn: pp. 14–15; Destruction
of Atlantis, English School, (20th century) / Private
Collection / © Look and Learn / Bridgeman Images:
cover; Corbis: Bettmann: p. 21; Leemage: p. 41; DK
Images: p. 8; Getty Images: De Agostini Picture
Library: p. 6; iStock: LindaMarieB: pp. 1, 22–23; Valerie
Loiseleux: p. 24; ahau1969: pp. 28–29; Shutterstock:
Algol: pp. 3, 44–45; Reinhold Leitner: p. 7; Atelier
Sommerland: p. 9; Andrey Burmakin: p. 9 (inset); zens:
p. 10; Christian Mueller: p. 11; Anastasios71: p. 13; S-F:
pp. 18–19; Masterovoy: pp. 20–21; Beth Swanson: p. 25;
Luis Santos: p. 26; cdrin: pp. 30–31; Renata Sedmakova:
p. 33; Panos Karas: p. 34; Viacheslav Lopatin: p. 36;
wjarek: p. 37; Elenarts: pp. 38–39; Cornfield: p. 40; Kiev.
Victor: p. 43; Algol: pp. 44–45; Topfoto: Fortean: pp.
4–5; World History Archive: p. 18; Wikimedia: p. 12;
Harrieta171/Pinpin: p. 27.

Library and Archives Canada Cataloguing in Publication

Hyde, Natalie, 1963-, author
    The lost city of Atlantis / Natalie Hyde.

(Crabtree chrome)
Includes index.
Issued in print and electronic formats.
ISBN 978-0-7787-2298-4 (bound).--ISBN 978-0-7787-2237-3
(paperback).--ISBN 978-1-4271-8091-9 (html)

    1. Atlantis (Legendary place)--Juvenile literature. I. Title.
II. Series: Crabtree chrome

GN751.H94 2016   j398.23'4   C2015-907964-0
                                           C2015-907965-9

Library of Congress Cataloging-in-Publication Data

CIP available at Library of Congress

Crabtree Publishing Company
www.crabtreebooks.com   1-800-387-7650

Printed in Canada/022016/MA20151130

Published in Canada
Crabtree Publishing
616 Welland Ave.
St. Catharines, ON
L2M 5V6

Published in the United States
Crabtree Publishing
PMB 59051
350 Fifth Avenue, 59th Floor
New York, New York 10118

Published in the United Kingdom
Crabtree Publishing
Maritime House
Basin Road North, Hove
BN41 1WR

Published in Australia
Crabtree Publishing
3 Charles Street
Coburg North
VIC 3058

Contents

Looking into the Past

Professor Richard Freund bent over the satellite photo. Beneath the mud, he could clearly see the shape of wide rings. There was another shape in the middle of the rings. It looked like a rectangle. Could this be the remains of a building?

▲ *People have been trying to find the lost island of Atlantis for centuries—but was it ever real?*

Lost Atlantis

Freund looked at his fellow scientists. Were they the rings of land and sea described in the legends? Was the rectangle the remains of a temple to the god Poseidon? Was the whole thing covered in mud because of a **tsunami**? If Freund's questions were true, then his team may have just found the lost city of Atlantis!

Poseidon was the ancient Greek god of the sea. In pictures he is often shown carrying a long fork with three prongs, called a trident. He was said to use this weapon to cause earthquakes.

tsunami: a huge sea wave caused by an underwater earthquake

Ancient Paradise

Atlantis was an island paradise said to have existed more than 11,000 years ago. It had high mountains, streams, and forests full of different animals. It also had plains with rich soil, so people could grow crops all year round. Valuable metals, such as gold and silver, were found in the ground.

▲ *The island of Atlantis was said to be home to a rich and powerful civilization.*

Land of Plenty

The island of Atlantis was divided into 10 kingdoms. Each kingdom had its own main city and was ruled by a powerful king. The island's great capital city was built on a hill and contained beautiful buildings and structures.

> "Now in this island of Atlantis there was a great and wonderful empire which had rule over the whole island."
>
> *Timaeus* by Plato

◀ *The island of Atlantis was controlled by the god Poseidon. The kings that ruled the kingdoms were* **descendants** *of Poseidon.*

descendants: people who are related to a particular ancestor

City of Circles

The capital city of Atlantis had an unusual design. It was surrounded by three rings of water with two circles of land in between. The rings of water were linked to the nearby sea by **canals**. The people used the sea to trade goods with other countries. Bridges connected the circles of land. The people built walls around each circle, with gates and towers to protect the city.

◀ *On the outer circles of land were buildings such as bathhouses and fountains. There was even a horseracing track.*

Shining in the Sun

In the middle of the city stood a royal palace built for Poseidon's wife, and a temple honoring Poseidon. They were richly decorated with silver, gold, and a rare metal called orichalcum. Inside the temple was a large gold statue showing Poseidon driving six winged horses. Around the outside of the temple were gold statues of all the kings and their wives.

▲ *The orichalcum metal in Atlantis was similar to bronze or brass.*

For centuries, orichalcum was only known about through ancient writings. In 2015, divers found the first samples of the metal on a ship that sank off the coast of Sicily 2,600 years ago.

canals: long, narrow channels filled with water

Atlanteans

The island of Atlantis was huge. Atlanteans lived both in the cities and on the plains. The people on the plains were farmers. Each farmer was given an area of land on which to grow crops and raise animals. In exchange for the land, the farmers promised to fight in the army during times of war.

▲ *In ancient civilizations such as Atlantis, all farm work was done by hand.*

"**They were not to take up arms against one another, and they were all to come to the rescue if any one in any city attempted to overthrow the royal house.**"

An oath taken by everyone who lived in Atlantis

▲ *Colored stones were placed in patterns to decorate the buildings.*

War and Peace

Artists, priests, and workers lived in the cities. The artists would decorate buildings, such as bathhouses, with patterns using different colored stones. Ancient writings say that the Atlanteans were an intelligent and peaceful people with a strong system of law in the beginning. Later, they became warlike and began **invading** surrounding areas.

invading: entering a region to take it over

A Forgotten Story

The story of Atlantis is said to have first been heard by a wise Greek lawmaker named Solon. Solon went to visit the priests of Sais, which is a region in Egypt. He knew they had ancient writings about the history of Greece. The priests told Solon an amazing tale. They said that the Greeks were descended from the people of Atlantis.

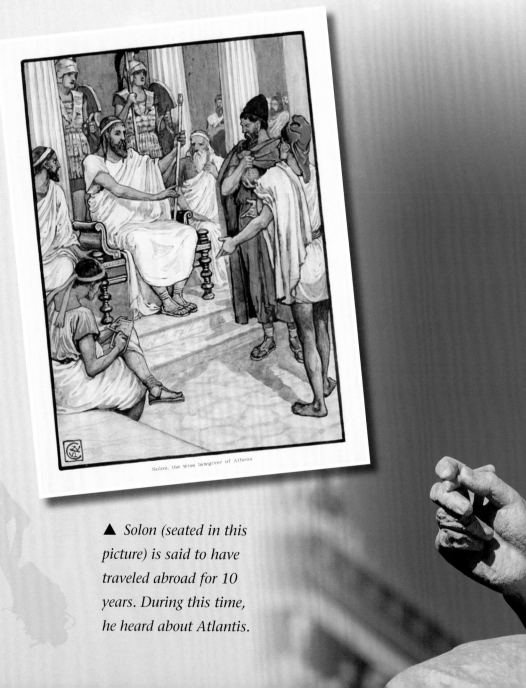

Solon, the wise lawgiver of Athens

▲ *Solon (seated in this picture) is said to have traveled abroad for 10 years. During this time, he heard about Atlantis.*

Spreading the News

Solon told people what he had heard when he returned to Greece. The story was passed down through generations. Eventually, the Greek **philosopher**, Plato, heard the tale. He included it in two of his books, *Critias* and *Timaeus*, which he wrote around 360 B.C.E.

◀ *For 2,000 years, everyone thought the island of Atlantis mentioned in Plato's books was just a made-up place.*

Plato lived from about 428 B.C.E. to 347 B.C.E. As a philosopher, he studied the world around him using logic and reason. He wrote many books and even opened his own school.

philosopher: a "thinker" who studies art and science

Know Your History

According to Plato, before the destruction of Atlantis, the Atlanteans began invading other territories and tried to rule them. The Athenian army from Greece fought against the Atlanteans and were able to defeat them. Plato wrote that when Solon visited the priests in Egypt, they scolded him for not knowing this history about his own country.

Write It Down

Records show that Solon did travel to Egypt during his life. Plato says that when Solon returned to Greece he tried to write the story as a poem. He found it too difficult and gave up. Plato decided to be the first to write down this forgotten piece of history.

"The large island of Atlantis had really existed and for many ages had **reigned** over all islands in the Atlantic sea."

Greek philosopher, Proclus

◄ *Plato writes that Solon tried and failed to tell the story of Atlantis.*

reigned: ruled over

Going, Going, Gone

The end of Atlantis was quick and violent. Plato writes that there were powerful earthquakes and floods. In "a single day and night," the land sank into the earth and Atlantis disappeared beneath the sea. He explained that this was why the sea in those parts could not be sailed.

Angry Gods

Plato believed that the gods were responsible for the terrible events. He wrote that they became angry because the once kind and peaceful Atlanteans changed. They grew greedy and warlike. The gods destroyed Atlantis as punishment.

▼ *The city of Atlantis and all its great buildings are said to have sunk beneath the waves.*

"Zeus, the god of gods [saw] that an honorable race was in a most **wretched** state, and [wanted] to inflict punishment on them..."

Timaeus by Plato

wretched: terrible or very bad

Can a City Really Disappear?

How could a kingdom as great as Atlantis suddenly just disappear? Scientists have found other places throughout history that were lost very quickly. Crete is an island in the Mediterranean Sea. The Minoan people lived there for thousands of years. Around the year 1400 B.C.E., a volcano on the nearby island of Santorini erupted. It caused earthquakes and a huge tsunami. The Minoan settlement on Crete was destroyed.

◀ *The eruption of a volcano on Santorini may have caused the tsunami that destroyed Atlantis.*

Gone in an Instant

Another city that was destroyed in a day is Pompeii, Italy. On August 24, 79 C.E., the volcano Vesuvius erupted. Poisonous gas and rock rolled down the volcano at 70 miles per hour (113 kilometers per hour). The city was covered in about 16 feet (5 meters) of hot ash and rock. It happened so quickly that thousands of people were trapped and died instantly. The city disappeared.

In 373 B.C.E., an earthquake and tsunami destroyed the city of Helike, Greece. The city was 1.2 miles (2 kilometers) away from the sea. It remains **submerged** to this day.

▼ *Pompeii was lost for over 1,500 years. It was found by accident in 1748.*

submerged: under water

Location, Location, Location

In 1881, a writer named Ignatius Donnelly suggested that Plato's story of Atlantis might be real. This sparked interest in people, and the hunt began. They thought that Atlantis was outside of Europe and Asia, and about 3,000 miles (5,000 kilometers) from Athens, Greece. It lay west of Egypt and central Italy. It was located "through the Pillars of Hercules," which may be another name for the Straits of Gibraltar.

▶ *The Rock of Gibraltar may be one of the "Pillars of Hercules" that Plato described.*

In 1664, the scholar Athanasius Kircher wrote a book about Earth's geography. He included information about Atlantis and a map showing where he believed it was located—in the middle of the Atlantic Ocean.

The Lost City

Plato tells us that Atlantis was bordered by a high mountain range. The city itself was beside the sea and surrounded by a large plain. It had **quarries** where black, white, and red stones were mined. There were also gold, silver, and precious gems in the area. One of the wild animals mentioned in ancient writings was the elephant.

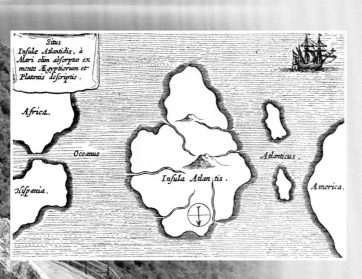

◀ No one is sure whether Kircher had clues to place Atlantis in the Atlantic Ocean or whether he just guessed.

quarries: deep pits where minerals are mined

Finding Atlantis

For years, researchers searched the clues in Plato's writings to come up with possible locations. Some thought that Atlantis was in Northern Europe. Others were sure it was in Antarctica. Still others believed it was beneath the waters of the Black Sea.

▶ *Many people believe that Atlantis is waiting to be discovered at the bottom of the Atlantic Ocean.*

Using Science

As time went on, people turned to science to help in the search. They studied early maps to see changes in coastlines. They dug in the ground for **artifacts**. They used new technology. Computer programs pinpointed likely sites. In the end, four strong possible locations remained.

▲ *This map shows the four most likely locations for Atlantis—the Bahamas, Crete, southern Spain, and Morocco.*

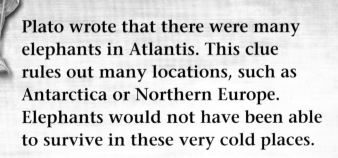

Plato wrote that there were many elephants in Atlantis. This clue rules out many locations, such as Antarctica or Northern Europe. Elephants would not have been able to survive in these very cold places.

artifacts: objects made by human beings

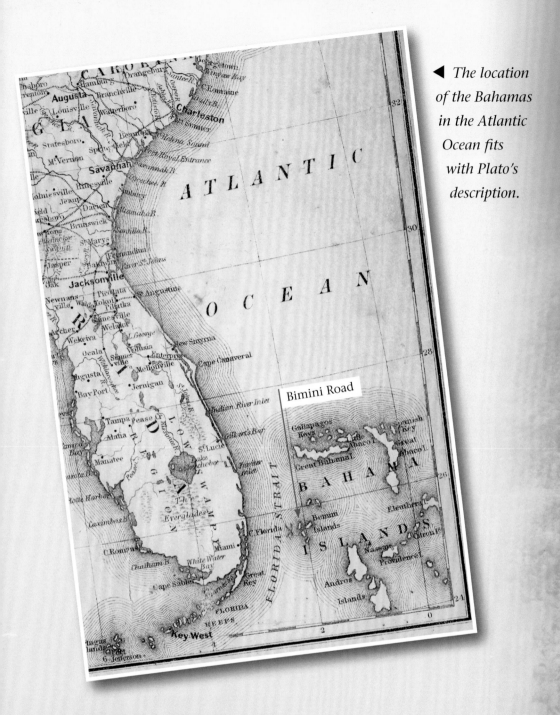

◀ *The location*
of the Bahamas
in the Atlantic
Ocean fits
with Plato's
description.

Bimini Road

The Bimini Road

There is something unusual off the coast of the
Bahamas in the Atlantic Ocean. A group of rocks form
what looks like an underwater road. Many of these
rocks seem to be rectangular, while natural rocks
tend to be round. Were these rocks shaped by human
hands? Was this road part of the sunken Atlantis?

For or Against?

Some researchers say the rock road is natural rock called **beachrock**, which has been broken into rectangular shapes over time. They say the rock is not old enough to have been part of Atlantis. But others point out that the Bimini Road stones are different from the beachrock in the sea nearby. They say this straight path under the water must be made by humans.

People who study Atlantis and believe it was a real place are sometimes referred to as Atlantologists. Many Atlantologists are convinced that the Bimini Road marks the site of the lost city.

beachrock: a type of limestone that forms in tropical regions

The Minoans on Crete

The island of Crete is another possible location of Atlantis. Some people believe that Plato was actually referring to the ancient Minoan settlement on Crete when he described Atlantis. There are many similarities. The Minoans were an advanced society. Their cities had paved streets and **sewage** systems. They decorated their buildings with colorful art. They were also a peaceful people.

▲ *The Minoans had beautifully decorated buildings like the Atlanteans.*

We know that the Minoans practiced bull-leaping. Plato records that the Atlanteans also did bull-leaping and describes how bulls were hunted in a ritual in the temple of Poseidon.

A Fiery End

Believers say that the eruption of the volcano on Santorini fits the story, too. This caused a huge tsunami to sweep over parts of Crete. Other people say that Crete was too small to be Atlantis. There is no evidence of rings of land and sea. Also, the Minoans did not build a temple to Poseidon. In fact, there are no temples at all on Crete.

▲ *In bull-leaping, someone would grab the bull's horns and when it raised its head, the person would leap off the ground and somersault over the bull's back.*

sewage: human waste that is carried away in drains and sewers

Doñana National Park

The coast of southern Spain, on the Atlantic Ocean, could also be the site of Atlantis. It lies through the Straits of Gibraltar, which are thought to be the "Pillars of Hercules." Scientists have found clues in the marshlands of Doñana National Park. Special **radar** shows faint circles in the ground. These are similar to the land and sea circles of Atlantis.

Into the Earth

The radar also picked out two rectangles under the ground. A team led by Richard Freund believes these may be the temple of Poseidon and the royal palace. This area has a history of tsunamis and floods. Could the remains of Atlantis be buried beneath the mud? Or are the rings and rectangles just natural formations in the earth?

▲ *Pieces of pottery found in the marshes of Doñana show that many different groups of people lived in this area for thousands of years.*

On the outskirts of the park, Freund and his team have found what they believe to be "memorial cities." They think these are places where survivors fled after the disaster that destroyed Atlantis.

radar: radio waves sent into the earth to show underground objects

Moroccan Atlantis?

Michael Hübner, from Germany, presented a new **theory** in 2008. He used a computer program to identify the location of Atlantis. He put in all the clues in Plato's writing. The computer came up with one answer: Morocco, Africa. South of the Moroccan city of Casablanca is the Souss-Massa plain. It fits almost all of Plato's descriptions.

▼ *Most of the 51 clues mentioned by Plato fit with the landscape of the Souss-Massa plain in Morocco.*

A Good Fit

Just as in Plato's story, the plain here is surrounded by mountains—the Atlas mountains. Streams run down from the mountains. There are red, black, and white stone quarries. There are elephants. There have also been tsunamis in this area. However, no scientific study has been done here yet. These could all be the same by accident.

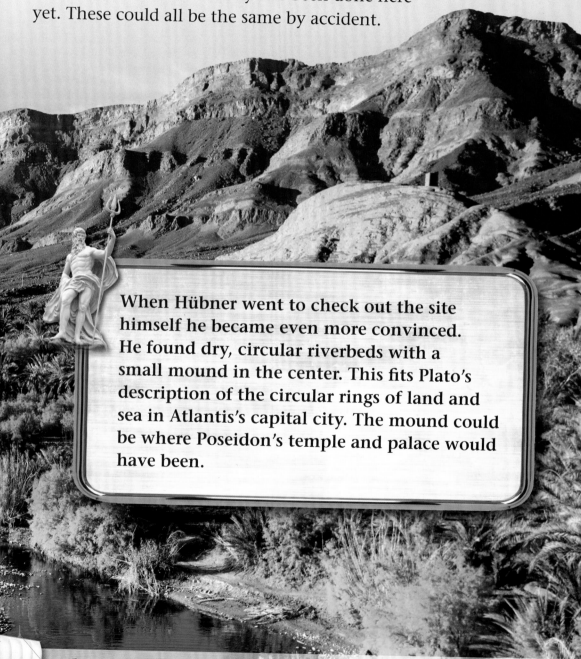

When Hübner went to check out the site himself he became even more convinced. He found dry, circular riverbeds with a small mound in the center. This fits Plato's description of the circular rings of land and sea in Atlantis's capital city. The mound could be where Poseidon's temple and palace would have been.

theory: an idea that has not been proved true

Problems, Problems...

Is the story of Atlantis true or not? Some people say it is, others say it isn't. Some argue that if Atlantis had been real, others would have written about it in Plato's time or even before. Plato says that Atlantis traded with many countries, yet no one has found records in other countries of these trades.

▲ *A canal linked Atlantis's capital city to the ocean. This allowed the Atlanteans to use ships to trade goods with other countries.*

◀ *Herodotus studied and wrote about the history of the Greeks. He is known as "The Father of History."*

Missing in History

Herodotus was a Greek **historian**. He lived about 100 years before Plato and traveled a great deal. Plato wrote of a great battle between the Atlanteans and the people of Athens. Herodotus does not mention this battle in his writings. Plato also stated that Atlantis was the biggest island in the world. Herodotus wrote that the biggest island was Sardinia.

After Plato, it was 300 years before someone else recorded any information about Atlantis. Diodorus Siculus was a Greek historian. In one of his books he described a tribe of people he called "Atlanteans."

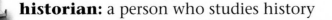

historian: a person who studies history

A Work of Fiction?

Some people say that Plato's story of Atlantis is just that—a story. He never meant for readers to believe in Atlantis. Plato's student, Aristotle, said that Plato made up the story to prove a point. He wanted to show what could happen to a peaceful people if they became greedy and bitter: their world could be destroyed.

▶ *Aristotle said that Plato's story was not real but was intended as a warning.*

Found in History

Other people think that the events Plato described were true, but he set them in a made-up place he called Atlantis. The tsunami of Helike may have **inspired** the tale of Atlantis's destruction. The war Plato describes could be based on Athens' invasion of the Italian island of Sicily.

▲ *The Athenian army suffered a terrible defeat at the invasion of Sicily in 415 B.C.E.*

> "He could create nations out of thin air and then destroy them."
>
> Aristotle, talking about Plato

inspired: caused someone to do something good

▲ *Plato's students were divided. Some believed Atlantis to be a real place.*
Others thought it was made up by Plato.

What He Said

A number of people believed that all of Plato's writings were
indeed true. Theophrastus was another student of Plato.
He disagreed with Aristotle. He wrote that the Atlantis story
was fact, not fiction. Greek historian Posidonius mentioned
Atlantis in his book on earthquakes. He said it was an
example of land swallowed by the sea.

Carved in Stone

Crantor was a Greek philosopher. He said that Atlantis was "straightforward history." He stated that the story was recorded in Egypt. He claimed to have heard from the priests in Sais that the story was carved on a pillar that stood in Egypt at that time.

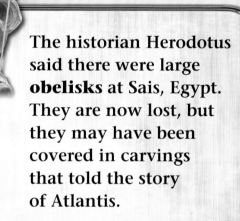

The historian Herodotus said there were large **obelisks** at Sais, Egypt. They are now lost, but they may have been covered in carvings that told the story of Atlantis.

◀ *Obelisks are often carved with symbols that tell of important events.*

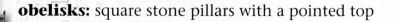

obelisks: square stone pillars with a pointed top

Is It Even Possible?

Timeline Troubles

Scientists believe they have a good idea of when humans learned and improved new skills over time. They know when people began farming instead of gathering food. They have figured out when humans began building cities and temples, and when they invented certain types of ships.

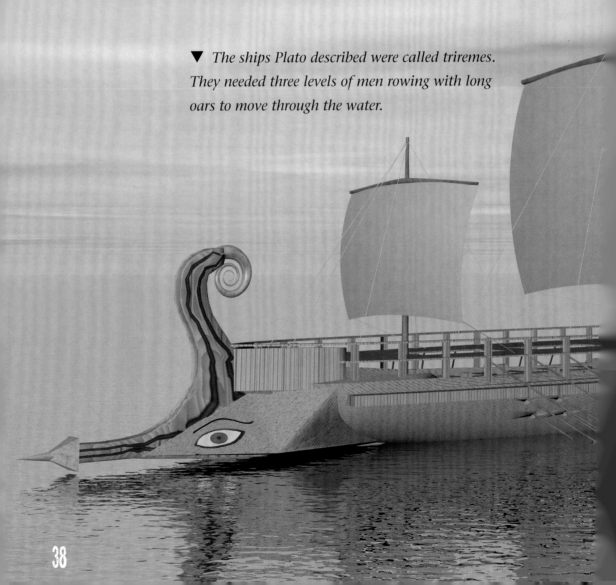

▼ *The ships Plato described were called triremes. They needed three levels of men rowing with long oars to move through the water.*

Row Your Boat

None of these dates fit with Plato's Atlantis. According to Plato, Atlantis existed 11,000 years ago. Scientists argue that this is before people began building temples, canals, or huge walls. At this time, humans were still making skin-covered boats or **rafts** to travel on water. The boats Atlanteans were said to be using were not invented for another 8,500 years!

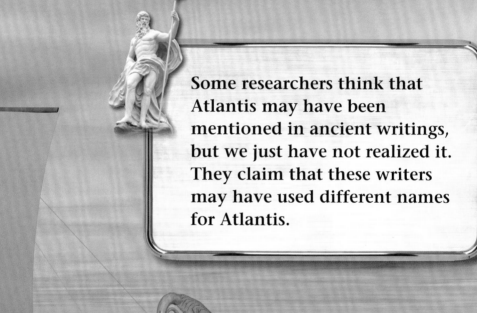

Some researchers think that Atlantis may have been mentioned in ancient writings, but we just have not realized it. They claim that these writers may have used different names for Atlantis.

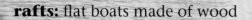

rafts: flat boats made of wood

Ancient Temple

Many researchers say that a city like Atlantis could have existed in 9000 B.C.E. They point to the temple of Gobekli Tepe in Greece. This temple was built around the same time as Atlantis. It has beautifully carved pillars, decorated with images of animals, that stand in the middle of walled stone circles.

▲ *The builders of Gobekli Tepe created pillars that are up to 6 feet (1.8 meters) high, and weigh up to 20 tons (18 metric tons).*

How Did They Do That?

This may prove that people were capable of building a city like Atlantis thousands of years ago. Even without metal tools, humans could create walls, canals, and temples. New discoveries are happening all the time. They show that we do not yet know everything about the things that early humans could do.

For centuries, everyone thought that the city of Troy in the book *The Iliad*, written by the greek poet Homer, was just a made-up place. But **archeologists** found the city of Troy in Turkey in 1870, proving it was in fact real.

▲ *Scientists found signs of fire and killing in the ruins of Troy. These match Homer's description of the Trojan War between Troy and Ancient Greece. It is said the Greeks won the war by entering Troy in a wooden horse.*

archeologists: scientists who study ancient people

Atlantis Today

Atlantis Lives On

The story of Atlantis is still popular today. It has found its way into hundreds of books, comics, movies, games, and music. Aquaman in DC comics was said to come from Atlantis. Many movies mention the lost island, including *Journey to the Center of the Earth* and Disney's *Atlantis: The Lost Empire*.

In the Bahamas and the United Arab Emirates, there are hotel resorts themed on the story of Atlantis. Both resorts offer a fun adventure through the lost city.

▼ *Disney's 2001 movie* Atlantis: The Lost Empire *tells the story of a young map-maker who discovers the ancient city.*

Underwater Setting

Many other stories also feature the lost city. In one of
K.A. Applegate's *Animorphs* series, the characters find
a civilization at the bottom of the ocean. Many video
games, such as *Age of Mythology*, are set in Atlantis.
Anime series such as *Nadia: The Secret of Blue Water*
pull from the story of Atlantis.

▲ *An underwater aquarium at Atlantis, The Palm, in the United
Arab Emirates, is scattered with the "ruins" of Atlantis.*

anime: a style of Japanese cartoon

Still Looking

Researchers are still hoping to find traces of the lost city. They are using advanced technology to help them. They are looking underground with special radar. Satellite images taken from space show possible locations. The oceans are being mapped with **sonar** readings. Today's science is giving us the best chance of locating Atlantis.

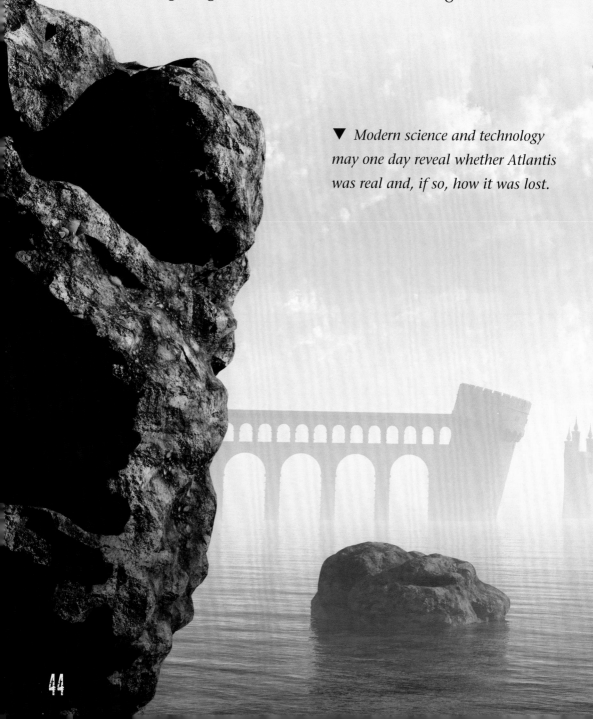

▼ *Modern science and technology may one day reveal whether Atlantis was real and, if so, how it was lost.*

Digging Deep

The orichalcum found off the coast of Sicily has sparked interest in Atlantis again. Mark Adams, who wrote about Hübner's theory of Atlantis in Morocco, is excited. He hopes scientists will take the idea seriously. He wants them to dig on the Souss-Massa plain. It might finally solve the mystery of the lost city of Atlantis.

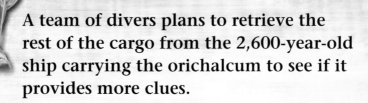

A team of divers plans to retrieve the rest of the cargo from the 2,600-year-old ship carrying the orichalcum to see if it provides more clues.

sonar: using sound to find objects under water

Books

The Mystery of Atlantis
by Kathryn Walker
(Crabtree, 2009)

Atlantis, the Lost City
(DK Readers)
by Andrew Donkin
(DK Children, 2000)

Atlantis: The Mystery of the Lost City
by Jack DeMolay
(Rosen, 2007)

Atlantis: The Legend of a Lost City
by Christina Balit
(Henry Holt, 2000)

Atlantis: The Search for the Lost City
by Mary-Jane Knight
(Kingfisher, 2012)

The Mystery of Atlantis
by Michael Martin
(Capstone Press, 2013)

Websites

http://channel.nationalgeographic.com/video/?tab=all&sort=recent&filter=all&q=atlantis
Videos by National Geographic on Atlantis.

http://news.nationalgeographic.com/2015/03/150318-atlantis-morocco-santorini-plato-adams-ngbooktalk/
Mark Adams talks about Huebner's theory of Atlantis in Morocco.

www.kidzworld.com/article/960-history-the-lost-city-of-atlantis
Facts and links for kids interested in digging further into the mystery from Kidzworld.

http://easyscienceforkids.com/all-about-the-lost-city-of-atlantis/
Fun facts and new vocabulary relating to Atlantis at Easy Science for Kids.

Glossary

anime A style of Japanese cartoon

archeologists Scientists who study ancient people

artifacts Objects made by human beings

beachrock A type of limestone that forms quickly in tropical regions

canals Long, narrow channels filled with water

descendants People who are related to a particular ancestor

historian A person who studies history

inspired Caused someone to do something good

invading Entering a region to take it over

obelisks Square stone pillars with a pointed top

philosopher A "thinker" who studies art and science

quarries Deep pits where minerals are mined

radar Radio waves sent into the earth to show underground objects

rafts Flat boats made of wood

reigned Ruled over

sewage Human waste that is carried away in drains and sewers

sonar Using sound to find objects under water

submerged Under water

theory An idea that has not been proved true

tsunami A huge sea wave caused by an underwater earthquake

wretched Terrible or very bad

Index

Entries in **bold** refer to pictures